Sarah Merriam Brooks

Across the Isthmus to California in '52

Sarah Merriam Brooks

Across the Isthmus to California in '52

ISBN/EAN: 9783337257378

Printed in Europe, USA, Canada, Australia, Japan

Cover: Foto ©Andreas Hilbeck / pixelio.de

More available books at **www.hansebooks.com**

ACROSS THE ISTHMUS

TO

CALIFORNIA

IN '52

BY

SARAH MERRIAM BROOKS

SAN FRANCISCO
C. A. MURDOCK & CO., PRINTERS
1894

ACROSS THE ISTHMUS

TO CALIFORNIA IN '52.

PART I.

I HAD been living in Boston three years—three years of the most exciting times, I think, which that city has ever experienced. I went in '49, and left in '52.

Theodore Parker, William Lloyd Garrison, Wendell Phillips, Emerson, and Lowell were all in the lecture field. Kossuth went there, and the question of intervention or non-intervention was brought up in the Senate and House, and speeches from the brightest minds were called out. Then came Jenny Lind to the music-lovers, and Anna Cora Mowatt to the theatre-goers. To the lovers of the exciting and horrible the Parkman murder gave plenty of material, not only there, but to the English-speaking world at large. Swedenborg's doctrines had taken root, and homœopathy was coming to the front, while women physicians, with Harriet K. Hunt at their head, were securing social recognition. Advance sheets of Dickens came over fortnightly, and little coteries of ladies were formed here and there to read them aloud. Afterwards came a most distracting discussion of the probable outcome of the story. The first School of Design was started in a small room over a store; and the first woman's rights convention — of Boston women mostly — was held in Worcester. Mesmerism and table-tippings were looking up, and clairvoyants were doing a thriving business, not only in diagnosing diseases, but in prescribing for them.

In those years the Republican party got its first recognition — not as a whole, but by getting a Locofoco plank inserted in a party platform. Webster was no longer the idol of the Whigs. His advocacy of the Fugitive Slave Law had deposed him, and the city went wild over the attempts to enforce that law.

A friend of mine was sitting quietly at her window opening on Bowdoin Square one day, when she saw a carriage driven in from Court Square, a block away. She had only time to notice this, when a black man, hatless and shoeless, assisted by two other black men, came running in from Court Square, and jumping into the carriage, were driven quick-

ly away. They were barely out of sight when
a crowd of people of all classes — police, civil-
ians, and many women — came whooping and
howling in from Court Square, in hot chase
after the black men. But they did not get
them! The man helped away was Shadrack,
the only fugitive slave who was publicly res-
cued from the workings of this law.

The next day being Sunday, Mr. Parker's
meeting-place (then the old Melodeon Music
Hall) was crowded to its utmost capacity with
people who were either sympathizers with him
in his opposition to the obnoxious law or were
curious to hear what he had to say of an act
which had set the city in a turmoil. He
opened the service by reading from a little
paper he held in his hand, that "Shadrack, a
fugitive slave, asked the prayers of this church
and all Christian people for aid in seeking his
liberty." After reading the note, amid the
most profound silence, Mr. Parker added:
"But this Shadrack *is* delivered from the
hands of his enemies!" Then such applause
went up from the people as it is impossible to
describe. It was quite against Mr. Parker's
desire that any applause should be allowed at
his services; but at this time full liberty was
given to the pent-up feelings of his hearers.

Indeed, I doubt if he thought he could help
it. After a while he gently raised his hands—
his way of enforcing silence—and went on
with his services as though nothing unusual
had happened. His friends felt that this was
his proper course. Others, who were in sympathy with the slave-holders, went away much
disappointed, because they expected a fiery
and denunciatory sermon, and only heard one
of love and charity to all mankind. To me
the whole scene was the most impressive I
had ever witnessed.

I had friends or acquaintances in every
movement going on, and no one could help
feeling an interest when every topic of conversation seemed to have an element of ex-
citement.

From such associations and surroundings I
was suddenly summoned to California. My
first thought was, "Impossible!" My next,
"Can I do it?" and the next, "Yes, this is
just what I want—a new land, a chance to
live what I have learned, to be an actor in the
world, and not a waiting soul." I had the
usual experience of persons about to under-
take what was then considered a difficult and
hazardous journey for a man,—how much
more for a woman with a little child only

three and a half years old! One said I ought
not to attempt such a thing; others wished
they had the chance, and still others saw all
sorts of dangers and disasters in my way. A
dear sister clung beseechingly to me, and only
gave way when she had exacted a promise
from me that in case I did not like the country, or there were hardships to endure, I would
come back in a year. I said "Yes," but I
thought "No—most decidedly no!" I resolved
to go forward, but never backward.

It took a long time then to arrange prelim-
inaries. It was midwinter when I decided to
go, and the 26th of April was the first date
on which I could secure tickets. Alvin Adams,
the king of expressmen, was a personal friend,
and he undertook the selection and purchasing of tickets, and doing all else that was
possible in advance for my comfort. He was
anxious I should go at that time, as the
steamers "Illinois" and "Golden Gate" were
advertised to make a trial trip then, and anything which promised a lessening in time of
the tedious journey was much to be desired.

For the first time he was sending a messenger through with his express matter, and that
gentleman was to look after me on both sides
of the Isthmus. But in crossing the Isthmus

I was to rely upon some one else, as he would
have all he could possibly do in looking after
his large business. Mr. Adams gave me an
order on Covy & Co., at Aspinwall, for especial
transportation for myself and escort, which
meant riding and baggage animals, and a
muleteer for our own use. How very valuable
it was to me will be seen later on.

After the matter of tickets was settled came
the next important one of trunks and wardrobe. A friend of mine had spent nine months
in California, and returned the previous fall.
He gave me full instructions about my baggage, which was all right; but when it came
to wardrobe, his ideas were somewhat confused.
He had spent most of his time in the moun-
tains, where it was exceedingly warm, but start-
ing home, had come through San Francisco,
and found it quite cool. People had told him
it was never warm there, and if he knew any
one going there to advise them to take only
thick clothing. So between his experience of
extreme heat and others of none at all, there
was room for doubt as to a proper selection.
Only one thing was very sure. That was, I
was to take only new clothes. Transportation
was so expensive it was useless to take any
which would not last until goods could be

sent there. I did the best I could with these
rather conflicting ideas, and took all the good
clothes for either hot or cold weather which I
was possessed of, and bought more, which I
thought might be needed. But oh, how I
longed for some old, or half-worn, or cheap
things on that long journey! Only in one
particular did I not follow any advice,—and
that was in my little daughter's wardrobe. I
had read how dirty a ship at sea could be;
and for her I took everything she had, however old it might be, and everything new that
I had room for.

My trunks were made expressly for the
trip (I have them now), and to be just a load
for a mule,— two trunks, and a bonnet-box
half their length, but otherwise the same.
They were made of light but strong wood,
covered with sheepskin, and bound with many
bands of steel. The trunks were to go on
each side of the pack-saddle, and the box on
top and between them; and the space left by
lack of length was to be utilized for anything
I might wish afterwards. Of the trunks, one
was for packing, with no compartments; the
other had a space divided off in the top and
one tray. The bonnet-box had only one tray.

It seems incredible to me now the amount

of clothing I put in those trunks. I began packing a month before I started, and as the contents settled, I filled in more. The night before I left, my trunks were locked; but the box was left open for those things which are sure to turn up at the last moment. Several friends came in during the evening bringing little gifts, and these were put in the tray with other light articles. In the lower part were eight bonnets, twenty-three pairs of under-sleeves — everybody wore undersleeves with every dress then, — besides collars, pocket-handkerchiefs, veils, and many other things which would not bear packing with heavy clothes. I mention these things now, as that box played quite an important part in my Isthmus experience.

The parting with my friends came at last, and while it seemed hard to them, there was no sadness in it for me. I felt brave, hopeful, and happy. My friend of California experience was to go with me to New York and see me safely on board ship. We arrived late Saturday night, and went to the Irving House. A drizzling rain had accompanied us during the afternoon, and had shut out all objects of interest which might have helped to pass the time during that tedious car ride. But a cheerful fire and a good supper made amends, and a sound sleep put us in spirits again.

Sunday my friend left me to visit a brother in Brooklyn. Lena being busy with her doll and picture-books, I felt rather at a loss for something to interest me, when I noticed a book which had been handed me by a friend who bade me good-bye at the depot in Boston. He gave it to me with the remark that it was a new book—just out, in fact,—dealing largely with a subject in which we were both much interested, and he thought I might like to read it on the steamer.

I meant to keep it for that purpose, but had read only a few lines when I became entirely absorbed in its pages. The book was a paper-covered edition of "Uncle Tom's Cabin." I read on until tears blinded my eyes. Then I realized this was no reading for one who had begun to experience the feeling of being a stranger in a strange land, and I resolutely shut the book and put it out of sight, so that I should not be tempted to take it up again—at least not while I was alone. I little thought then how much in touch my feelings were with a waking world—awaking to the awful importance of the Slavery question, which came so near wrecking our Union.

While at breakfast that morning I thought I had noticed some peculiar movements about the waiters in the dining-hall. I fancied there was whispering among them, and rather pointed observation of me. I asked my friend if it was so, and if so, why? He said the direction on my baggage had been noticed, and he had been asked if I did not want an attendant; that I could have one on my own terms, if I could secure a passage for one. Now, going down to lunch alone, I was approached by one of the waiters, a fine-looking mulatto, who made a similar offer. He would serve me on the journey, and work for me after getting to California for any time I might name, if I would just take him there. As servants could go for half fare, the offer seemed tempting, but one which I had to decline, as also that made by one of the girls, in almost the same words. The desire of this class to get to California was so great they would promise almost any terms to accomplish that end.

My experience afterwards proved that very few who took them at their word got any benefit from them. They would promise to work for a certain length of time in payment for their passage-money, and when they got through would desert at the first offer of increased wages. There was no way to keep them to their word, and servants were so scarce that few people were above getting them away, even from a friend, if doubling or trebling their wages would do it.

The "Illinois" was to sail Monday afternoon, April 26th. We went down early to avoid the rush, if possible; but there was no avoiding that with all the people who were to go. The crowd pushed and pulled, shouted and swore, and somehow we got on board, and halted in a sort of ante-saloon. With my wraps and satchels disposed around me, I waited for my friend to find my berth. He was gone so long that I began to feel somewhat anxious, when he returned with the information that the stateroom as a whole was taken and occupied by a party from New York. How could this be possible, I said, when there was my ticket, calling for the lower berth in stateroom K, first cabin, one of the very best on the steamer? Mr. Adams had taken great pains to get this particular berth, for which I had paid three hundred and fifteen dollars, and here I was with apparently no berth at all.

The noise and confusion, the ringing of bells, the shouting of all to come aboard, and finally the orders for all visitors to go on shore, so upset me that I made no remonstrance when my friend told he me had given my ticket to the purser, who had assured him I should be comfortably provided for as soon as the bustle had a little subsided. He bade me good-bye, and was gone before I fully realized that I had nothing to show that I had paid my fare and was entitled to my berth. At first I felt dismayed, and then a little angry, at my situation. I had travelled thousands of miles alone without a mishap; and here I was supposed to be under the care of a competent escort, and yet left in a most awkward position.

I do not know how long I sat where my friend left me; but matters had quieted down, everybody seemed to have got their berths, and still I was there. At last the stewardess came along and asked me why I was there. I said I was waiting to find out, and if she would ask the purser, perhaps *she* would find out. After a while she came back with word that I could have a berth in stateroom K, second cabin, for the present, and afterwards some other arrangement might be made. But no other arrangement ever was made, and all my efforts to that end were fruitless. I could not get the purser to see me, and any appeal

to the captain was answered by referring me
to the purser.

I found out later on that this was not an
uncommon occurrence. Some one in New
York resold staterooms, and trusted to getting
their people on board before the fraud was
discovered and too late to make any trouble about it. Generally, it was perfectly safe
to do this,— for in the scramble and anxiety
of people to get to California, a little thing
like being cheated out of a berth, and having
to sleep on a table or the floor, didn't count
for much with single men, and usually they
were the sufferers. When I wrote back to
Mr. Adams of my experience, he went on to
New York and had an overhauling of the
business. Many wrongs of this kind came to
light, and after this some safeguard was placed
around ticket-holders so they were sure of
getting what they had paid for. Who pock-
eted the money obtained by double and triple
selling of tickets was never found out, as far
as I know.

After being fully convinced that nothing
could be gained by holding out for my rights
any longer, I followed the stewardess to the
berth allotted me in the second cabin. This
second cabin had a row of staterooms around

the side, the centre being entirely taken up by
standees, each having two cots, entirely without pillows or bedding. The occupants were
supposed to provide for themselves in that
respect. I was shown to stateroom K, and
found it so fully occupied there seemed no
room for me. Upon interviewing the persons there, I found we had all been treated
alike. We were entitled to stateroom K, first
cabin, but had been ousted by the "party
from New York." There were two berths and
a sofa in our stateroom, and we soon came to
an amicable arrangement about places. The
woman with two children took the lower berth,
the other woman with one child took the sofa,
and I took the upper berth with my little girl.

As soon as we had arranged our belongings
to the best advantage, we went to the saloon
for our supper, the bell having rung while we
were getting settled. We had taken only a few
mouthfuls when a sea struck us, and some of
those who had outside seats were landed on
the floor. Those who had divan seats fared
better, but with stomachs too unsteady to stay
longer at the table. We were told we were off
Sandy Hook, and might expect rough sailing
for some time. I took Lena and found my
way to my room, too sick to do anything but

creep into our berth, as we thought for a little while, but which neither of us left for two days and nights. Occasionally I would rouse a little and look around, only to see every available spot in the room occupied with all kinds of food and liquids, which had been ordered by my roommates, hoping thereby to tempt a seasick appetite. Every opening which could let in a breath of fresh air was hermetically sealed. Let those who have suffered at sea imagine the result! During this time we had only once some gruel brought us, of which we ate very little, and now, the third morning out, were completely exhausted and consumed with thirst.

We had come into the Gulf Stream, and, of course, a much warmer climate, and found the garments we left New York in anything but comfortable. I was wondering whether I should make an effort to get up and dress, or lie quiet and just die easy—an event which seemed very likely to happen,— when I was conscious of an unusual noise and loud talking about our door, and then a demand for admission. One of the women answered, and then brought me a card, which proved to be that of my escort on the steamer, Mr. Adams' express messenger.

It seemed that as soon as he had taken care of his business that first night out, he began to look for us. Some one told him persons answering our description had been taken sick at the supper-table and had gone to their berth. As this was to be expected, he thought no more of it that night. The next day the same answer was given; but when the second day passed and we did not appear, he became anxious, and now, the third morning out, began a personal search, which resulted in his appearance at our stateroom. He urged me to get on deck, if possible, fearing if I stayed longer in that close atmosphere I would bring on a fever.

I told him if I could have the room to myself for half an hour, the unpleasant accumulation removed, and the port opened, I might possibly manage it. As my roommates had been in possession of all the available space except my berth during the two days and three nights, I did not consider my request unreasonable. But although it was granted, I realized I had given offence. My first move was to open the port and transom and let in the blessed pure air, which of itself was enough to revive one. Lena was delighted at the prospect of getting out of that dreary

room, and as soon as I had made her present-
able Mr. E—— took her on deck. By going
slowly and taking an occasional rest, I accom-
plished a sponge-bath—mostly cologne—and
got into more comfortable clothes. When thus
far along, I was in doubt of being able to as-
cend the stairs; but upon opening the door
found my escort and a friend waiting to help
me on deck. There I found a standee, with
pillow and blanket, and the stewardess waiting with a dish of rice and an ice-cold drink.

When Lena and I had eaten and drunk,
I quite gave up the idea of dying just then.
There was an awning over that part of the
deck, but lying there on the cot, my eyes
seemed on a level with the ocean, which
looked bright and glorious in the morning
sun. Every breath I drew gave me life and
strength, and I began to feel an interest in
my surroundings. There were several standees around, occupied by those who had been
seriously ill, and could gain no strength while
confined to their berths.

I had only been on deck a short time when
a gentleman came to the standee next mine
and said something to the lady lying there.
I recognized him at once as having been head
salesman in a large dry-goods establishment

in Boston, where I had done much of my purchasing. As soon as he saw me, he gave me a cordial greeting and then introduced me to his wife, a lovely woman, who had been cruelly seasick, and was still unable to leave her cot. From that time on, no brother and sister could have been kinder. They were going to Stockton, he having bought a partnership in a wholesale grocery business, intending to stay there two years, and then return to a home in New England, which he had lately purchased.

I wish to say here that of all the people whom I met who were going to California for " two years and for a certain sum of money," —and their name was legion — he and one other were the only persons who, to my knowledge, lived up to their intention. Two years after our journey he and his wife called on me in San Francisco, while on their way home. He had made ten thousand dollars, the sum he went for, had no love for the country, and was going back perfectly satisfied with his venture. The other man was from Ohio, and one of a family of very pious people. He went into the mines, and, being handy with tools, made "cradles" for washing gold. He could make one in a day, for which he re-

ceived an ounce in gold-dust. He stayed
until he made much more than the sum he
went for, and, I believe, got frightened, fearing
if he did not keep faith with himself something might happen to him. He also went
home perfectly satisfied to have escaped with
his money and his life from a civilization so
wild and rough as was found in a mining-
camp. A few days ago this gentleman called
on me. He was making a visit to California
for his health. I reminded him of what he
had told me of his object in coming here.
"Yes," he said, "I came for a purpose,— and
there she sits over in that chair," pointing to
a sweet-faced, gray-haired lady opposite me,
his good wife, and the mother of several children. How strange it all seemed!

My first day on the steamer deck was full of
wonder to me. I had heard of the crowded
steamers, but had no conception of what it
meant until that day. In the second cabin,
coming up, in the first cabin, looking through
as I came up the stairs, on deck, everywhere, a
crowd! Men, women, and children of all na-
tions seemed to have a representation more or
less numerous. At first all were mixed in
one confused mass; but after a while I became accustomed to the moving throng, and

thought I could single out some of my own country people. The impression of a crowd was not to be wondered at,— for, although the steamer was allowed only twelve hundred passengers, we were told, and every one believed it, there were fully sixteen hundred, counting stowaways, extra deck-hands, and smuggled-in steerage passengers. Those who occupied first or second cabins were allowed on deck at all times; but a portion of it was roped off once a day for an hour or two, when the steerage passengers could come up and enjoy the fresh air. At such times the cabin passengers "generally went below."

The first day was spent on my cot, and at night Mr. E—— proposed I should sleep there next his wife, while he swung his hammock just above us, and where he could reach us, in case he was needed in the night. This was altogether delightful to both Lena and myself, as we dreaded that fearful berth. There were a great many others who slept on deck — in fact, everybody who could,— for it was much pleasanter than a stuffy stateroom. Those who could not have a standee camped on the seat which ran along the edge of the deck, and others, wrapped in their blankets, slept on the floor for at least part of the night. All of these were routed out by daylight by the men who came to wash down the decks; but those who were in standees could remain until the decks were dry. After a few days the standees were discarded—as everybody was able to sit up and go to meals—until night, when many were brought up and occupied by those who were fortunate enough to secure them.

Lena had found pleasant companions, and was gay as a bird. Neither then nor afterwards was she the least trouble to me; and I attributed many of the kindnesses I received to her loving and dainty ways, which attracted most of our companions. I had heard men so often refer to children as unmitigated bores in travelling that I had felt somewhat anxious on her account where all were strangers. But I can truly say that never once was I made uncomfortable on her account, or was she snubbed. On the contrary, after we became a little acquainted with people, I was often asked for the "loan of her for a while," and she was brought back with a report of good conduct and a desire for her company again. Upon my expressing some surprise at this to a gentleman, he remarked that most children would be liked and all tolerated, if their faces and hands were kept clean, and they were made to mind their own business. I thought there was a sermon in that for all mothers.

Having occupied a standee for several nights, I thought myself equal to taking my berth again. Upon going down to prepare it in some measure, I found it had been used during that day by a preacher for the purpose of taking a wet pack to break up a fever. He was a friend of my roommates, and a doctor among the passengers had prescribed that treatment. As I had only gone down twice a day for a few moments, they felt justified in making such good use of my berth. I quite fell in with their idea, and gave up all further claim to it, only using the stateroom for toilet purposes when the others were on deck.

Now, that we were all well, making acquaintances was next in order, and from introductions to friends of Mr. Eastman, I soon had a number of pleasant companions. I found this trial trip of the "Illinois" and "Golden Gate" had been looked forward to and planned for by a party of old Californians who had spent the winter in the East, and were now returning. Later on, I found they were rather notable people; but then I knew them only as gentlemen kind and attentive to a stranger, and anxious to make the time pass pleasantly. All had stories to tell of themselves or the new country which I was soon to know, and which seemed charming to me, an eager listener.

Tom O. Larkin told of Monterey and southern ranches. He had a famous watch-chain of black pearls, and could tell some bit of history connected with each one. Benjamin Kendig went to California in '49, stayed one year, and returned to New Orleans. He fitted out a ship with merchandise and sent it to sea, with his son, twenty-three years old, as supercargo. Nothing was ever heard of the vessel, and Mr. Kendig was on a journey—round the world, if need be,—in hopes of finding some trace of his son. Tom Cahill—"Genial Tom," they all called him,—placed his big bamboo chair (which he slept in nights) at my disposal during the day. It could be elevated or lowered to any angle desired, and was a most luxurious resting-place. He had been in San Francisco during the two great fires, in one of which a dear brother perished before his eyes. Many a sigh came from him when others around were careless and happy, and we knew what thought caused it. Isaac Friedlander had gone to California in '49. He was so homesick he could not stay; but after being home two years was more sick to get back again. Speaking of his life in Charleston, South Carolina, he mentioned a firm to which he felt particularly indebted for kindness and assistance in his early business career. The men comprising that firm were my uncles, and I mentioned the fact, which seemed to greatly please him, and he assured me nothing would gratify him more than to be of service to Lena or myself during our journey. Mr. Cavalier, a French gentleman, made many efforts to be agreeable, but as he spoke little English and I less French, our attempts at conversation were a source of much merriment to all of us. There was another person who was a rather prominent Californian. He kept much to his stateroom, and no one seemed anxious for his society. The man was Sam Brannan, a person of great wealth and position in San Francisco for many years. He entertained largely in his stateroom, and at times became very hilarious, and had to be remonstrated with rather severely.

Among passengers from New York on a visit to San Francisco, was Wilkes, of the *Spirit of the Times* and *Police Gazette*. I made his acquaintance through Dr. Mott, a son of old Dr. Mott of New York, but of world-wide fame. Mr. Wilkes seemed quite a pleasant person, until one day I made confession that I had

never read a *Police Gazette!* To correct this
lack of intelligence, he brought me an armful
the next time he came on deck. I pitied his
apparent sorrow when I declined to read them,
and I am sure it was beyond his comprehen-
sion—such a lack of appreciation of what to
him was first-class literature. Of Fernando
Wood, it was said he was going out to exchange a hundred thousand dollars' worth of
New York property for a like value in San
Francisco with Tom O. Larkin. I do not
know if this was so, or only steamer gossip.

Among all our passengers there were only
eighty women and children; but this was by
far the largest number which had ever crossed
at one time. When the dangerous nature of
the journey is considered, and the fact that
most of the men were fortune-hunters, who expected to make that fortune in two years, the
small number of women and children is not to
be wondered at. In that number, however, we
had all kinds—the gentle invalid, who was *so*
nervous!—the large, jolly one, who, sitting
bolt upright, with her arms crossed on her
capacious bosom, and arrayed in a loose gown
of immense pattern, made fun for everybody;
my Lady Vere de Vere, who in dignified state
sat in lofty silence apart from the motley crowd.

Two representatives of the world of fashion occasionally came out of retirement, and gazing around for a while, seemed to be oppressed with that "tired feeling" which at the present time is a distinctive feature of fashionable life. They had been to Europe; and as that was a much more uncommon affair then than it is now, perhaps it accounted for the *blasé* appearance which they so much affected.

One of another class there was, with three of her chattels; but they kept so closely to themselves we knew nothing of them. But crossing the Isthmus she found a poor German and his wife dying with fever by the roadside, with two little children crying beside them. While others passed them by, this poor soul had them put on a litter and taken into Panama. There they died, and her money gave them decent burial in consecrated ground. Then putting the little ones into clean garments, albeit not the best of fits, she took them on the steamer, and shared her room with them. Whenever their clothing got dirty she made bold to ask of mothers to give of their abundance to the orphans, and was seldom refused. She took these children to San Francisco, and placed them with good German people, and saw that they were well brought up

and educated. A sum of money was placed
in such a way as to provide for all this, but
they never knew from whom it came. Would
my Lady Vere de Vere have done that?

One of my roommates was a plain, good
woman, happy in the thought of joining husband and father, and the hope that the climate
would make him a strong man again. The
other was the wife of a street contractor in
San Francisco. He had made much money,
and invested a portion of it in specimen quartz
jewelry. She had a chain of great length,
reminding one of Dick's hat-band, which we
are told went three times round and tucked
under. Pins, rings, and buckles, all of specimen jewelry, and all worn morning, noon, and
night, made her a rather conspicuous person.

Another woman brought her little girl, who
after we crossed the Isthmus developed a case
of measles, the germs of which were sown
broadcast before we knew what was the trouble. Many a left-handed blessing was cast
after the unwitting offender after we landed
in San Francisco. Some were going to the
mines; others were waiting their arrival at
San Francisco to know where or what was
their destination. But why go on? Each
and every one had a hope or expectation as

widely different as was their past and present life.

One of the first things I did after I got over my seasickness was to finish reading "Uncle Tom's Cabin." From the time I opened the book it became an object of interest to many people. The steamer was officered by Southern people, and nearly all with whom I became acquainted were more or less in sympathy with the South. It was not strange then that my book and I came in for a goodly share of curiosity. I could not stop reading a moment but some one would want to look at it, "just to see what it was like." Of course, no one could read a few words without wishing for the whole, and I was besieged with requests for it from would-be borrowers. I was perfectly willing to lend it; but soon realizing the strong feeling it was creating, I made each one who took it personally responsible for its safe return. This became necessary from the number who were waiting their turn, and I thought it prudent to keep a close watch upon it. Whenever it was returned some discussion followed. There was no attempt to lessen its merit as a book, but a great diversity of opinion as to its truthfulness in depicting plantation life. While I was not afraid to express my belief on the subject, I shunned argument, feeling it would be extremely unpleasant to create antagonism to me personally and could do no good to the cause. The consequence was all talked freely and good-naturedly on the subject, and I got nothing worse than a little raillery and being alluded to as the "Boston Abolitionist." How true my fears were for the safety of my book was proven later on. The last morning we were on the steamer it was taken out of my satchel in my stateroom while I was eating breakfast, and I never heard of it afterward.

The last few days on the Atlantic side were anything but pleasant,—for the weather had become uncomfortably warm and several cases of fever had developed, which, in our crowded condition, created anxiety.

As we neared the Isthmus, the interest of all centred in that much-dreaded part of our journey. The papers had given accounts of the dangers to be met with there—of robbers, loss of baggage, of people being left behind and having to wait for another steamer; and, worst of all, getting the much dreaded Panama fever. We knew transportation facilities were much improved; still we believed there was trouble of some sort ahead for us all. How

the eighty women and children were to be
disposed of when it came to mule carriage was
matter for much speculation.   One woman
going to Salem, Oregon, had eight children,
ranging from a young man of nineteen to an
infant in arms.   Some one asking her what
she expected to do with them when she came
to the mules, she said she expected to find
out when she did come to them, and not before.   Anyway she was not going to worry
about it.   The rest of us took the hint, and
there were fewer questions asked after this.
Dr. Mott had kindly offered to take care of
Lena and myself, and seemed to fear more for
our baggage than anything that might happen to us.   He had, beside his ordinary trunk
of clothing, a case of surgical instruments,
which would be extremely valuable to him in
San Francisco, if he could get them there in
good condition.   I showed him my order on
Covy & Co., at Aspinwall, which Mr. Adams
had given me, but told him candidly that after
my experience about my berth I did not know
as any order from him would be respected.
He thought it would be, and felt very hopeful
about it, and some others to whom he spoke
were sure it would be of great benefit to us.

PART II.

WE left the steamer at Aspinwall in the early morning, and walked to the cars in a drizzling rain. There were nine miles of railroad completed, but there was nothing yet done for the comfort of passengers—no depot or waiting-room. But what a ride and what a work the construction of that nine miles had been!

When I first got in the car there was a terrible crowd, and not seats for half the people. It seemed as if some one or many must be crushed. A gentleman who was in the car before we came gave me his seat, and then picked up Lena and put her in my lap. Seeing me interested in everything about us, he answered patiently and with apparent pleasure my innumerable questions about the country and people. He introduced himself by telling his name and position, which was a guarantee for the truthfulness of his information. He was Mr. Stevens, chief engineer in the construction department of the road.

First we talked of the difficulties of the

work. They had driven piles in many places
sixty feet deep, to get a foundation for the
sleepers. It seemed there was nothing but
decomposed vegetation as far down as that.
Then the difficulty with laborers was very
great,—for no one could work longer than a
week in that fever-laden air. If a man did
not leave then and fill up on quinine, he died ;
and most of them died anyhow. If the fever
was broken up, they took a cough which usually developed into quick consumption, and
that was the end of them. Mr. Stevens said,
and I heard it from others afterward, that a
double row of these dead men could have been
laid on the whole of that nine miles.

This gentleman was an enthusiastic bot-
anist, and never once wearied of my many
questions concerning the wonderful flowers
and ferns which were in bewildering profusion
everywhere. Huge trees bore aloft great ban-
ners of moss and flung out trails and vines of
brilliant parasites. It seemed as if the ground,
burdened with its wealth of verdure, was
sending up emissaries to make a second world
of loveliness on the sunny tree-tops. I have
never visited a fine conservatory since without
seeing many a plant and flower which I saw
there growing in wildest luxuriance. All were

not handsome, however; two were positively
wicked-looking, and I was not surprised to
learn they were very poisonous.

At the end of the nine miles of railroad,
we came to the Chagres river, where we were
to take boats for the next stage of our journey.
It took some time to get started,—for we had
to select our baggage and see it on the boat in
which we were to go.   Our boat took twenty
people and this baggage, which was piled in
the centre, in a sort of pyramid.   The boat
was a flat-bottomed affair, with a seat which
ran all round the inner edge.   The outer edge
was provided with a wide board, which served
as a sort of promenade, as it were, for the
boatmen.   They had long poles, which they
stuck from the prow of the boat into the bot-
tom of the river, and held there while they
trotted back, and the boat glided along under
their feet the length of the pole.   Running
forward again, they repeated the performance.

We had eight of these boatmen—big, black
fellows, almost naked.   Desperately ugly in
looks, they proved equally so in character.
It was about nine o'clock when we were fairly
under way.   For the first hour or so it was
cool, and the river was shaded by trees.   Then
the sun came out with a fierce heat, which

caused the perspiration to pour off the boatmen in copious streams, and eventually to
make them discard their solitary garment.

Almost every one was provided with thick
umbrellas, for protection from the sun, as well
as the showers, which were frequent and un-
expected. We would see a little thick, white
cloud, not unlike a bit of cotton, sailing in the
sky; and when it was over our heads it just
tipped up, and, after giving us a shower-bath,
passed serenely on. Then we steamed in the
heat of the sun, and, after being dried, were
consumed with fever.

People resorted to all sorts of things to
quench their thirst. Some took "fire-water,"
in any quantity or quality they had in private
stock. Some provident ones had coffee pre-
pared for them before leaving the steamer,
and now drank it nearly all at once, and
thirsted more than ever. One elderly person
had a bottle of pickled onions along, of which
he partook freely, and then drank the vinegar!
Some dipped up the water from the river and
drank, and repented ever after, for it had a
way of "cottoning" up in the mouth that was
intolerable. I had read somewhere that wet-
ting the wrists would allay fever. So when I
could bear the thirst no longer, I tried putting

my arm over the side of the boat for a few
moments, and found it a great relief. Soon
everybody was doing the same, and after this
there was less resorting to the bottle.

When our boatmen discarded their small
amount of clothing the female portion of our
company sought the seclusion of their umbrellas, whereupon the gentlemen commanded the
boatmen to resume their garments. A stormy
scene ensued, with the result that at the first hut
we came to on the bank of the river our men
deserted and left us to our fate. Their excuse
was they wanted breakfast; but after waiting
an hour for them, and being nearly suffocated
with heat, a delegation of well-armed men
sought them out, and found them fast asleep
under the trees. They were yelled at and
prodded with sticks, but being half drunk, it
was hard work to waken them. After much
threatening with knives and pistols, they sul-
lenly came down to the boat, with our men
bringing up the rear, with their weapons very
much in evidence. They were an ugly set,
and were constantly inventing excuses for
tying up at every hut that promised a drink
or snooze, which necessitated a constant watch-
fulness on the part of our men.

The terrible day wore on, and as the shadows

lengthened a little breeze came up, which made
it possible to breathe with some comfort. At
sunset we reached Taverneer, where we were
to spend the night. The boat was run up on
a little gravelly beach, and we all got out so
cramped, sore, and miserable altogether as to
make walking, even the short space required,
almost an impossibility. We were here to get
supper, lodging, and breakfast.

Taverneer consisted of two log houses. One
was the tavern proper: the other a place where
the sick men were sent when no longer able to
work on the railroad. If any one ate of that
supper, I did not know it,—for all were suffer-
ing for an opportunity to loosen their clothes
and stretch their limbs after the long confine-
ment in one position. This we were not allowed
to do until all had a chance to eat their supper; and as there were people enough to oc-
cupy the tables several times replenished, it
took a long while.

At last a man took a candle and beckoned
us to the side of the room, where were slats
nailed to the logs, forming a rough ladder, and
we were expected to climb these slats to our
sleeping-rooms! We looked at each other in
dismay, and asked how we were to do it. The
serving-man could not speak a word of Eng-

lish, and we no Spanish; so there we were huddled together at the foot of the ladder—if those slats were worthy that name—waiting for something to turn up. Soon the men came along, having been told that was the way to *their* sleeping-room. So they literally lent a hand, and by giving us one and using the other to pull themselves up, we managed the ascent. There was always one man between two women, to help in case of a misstep or lost grip. After we were all up, the men looked around for their separate quarters, and, lo and behold! there was only the one garret for us all. This seemed a dilemma, surely; but by this time we were "in for it," and had to take anything that came our way; and the less we grumbled the better.

The beds were single cots—no pillows, blankets, or bedding of any kind. There were not enough cots for even the women and children; so the men had to take the floor. I believe every man who crossed the Isthmus had provided himself with a pair of blankets, and many women also, or a heavy shawl, which answered the same purpose. Some of the men took their blankets and went down, thinking it would be pleasanter to sleep under the trees. They soon returned, however, concluding any shelter was better than the night air and the innumerable insects buzzing about.

Among our number were some young Germans who had a stock of diamonds and jewelry with them. They were determined not to lose sight of their baggage for a moment; so some were always on the watch, while the others got a few winks of sleep. There was a tarpaulin over the baggage, and some of our party crept under it and slept there.

The crying of children with fever and thirst, and the sick men who had persisted in drinking all sorts of "fire-water," contrary to the advice of those who knew better, made night hideous. The elderly person who had eaten so freely of pickled onions and drank the vinegar awoke from a troubled sleep with a whoop and a howl, and made haste for the one window, where he delivered up to Mother Earth her own again—and felt better.

The chattering of monkeys, the shrieks of night-owls, and every form of expression possible for paroquets, mocking-birds, and the like, beside many others of which we had no knowledge, made that night at Taverneer one to be remembered, but a repetition of which could hardly be desired. It seemed as if every tree in that dense forest by which we were sur-

rounded was the home of beast or bird and
teeming with life which had hidden away or
slept during the heat of the day. *Then* the
woods were as silent as though every living
thing was struck dumb. Add to this the coughs
of the sick men in the other log house, and the
experience was not conducive to rest or sleep.

I sat on the floor as long as I could, and
then tried lying on the cot at Lena's feet, with
a bag for a pillow. Then giving up in despair
of rest, went to the window to look out on that
strange night, and take in its, to me, wonderful aspects. The moon was shining brightly,
throwing shadows everywhere; and if anything
had been lacking in the reality of the weird
scene, the fancy could easily fill the void.

While I was thus musing, a pistol-shot star-
tled us all and filled us with alarm. Some of
the men went on a tour of inspection, and returned with word that a man in the boat shot
off his pistol, just to let people know he was
watching all right. I was told afterwards that
he saw a head of some kind peering over the
edge of the boat, and shot at it. He heard
nothing from it, and did not know what it
was; nor did he care, I imagine. If it was a
robber, all right; if a beast, all right. It was
not worth thinking about, anyway.

As soon as it was daylight, we gathered our belongings and descended from our sleeping-quarters in the same order in which we ascended the night before; but being rather more conspicuous in the morning light than by a tallow dip, we did not accomplish it quite so complacently. Our breakfast was a repetition of supper, with the addition of coffee, which was a veritable godsend; and we took the precaution to buy some crackers, which I really think saved our lives that day.

The first of our ride that morning was through much the same scenery as the day before; but that which so charmed us then became exceedingly monotonous now. Tree, fern, and flower failed to draw our minds from our exhausted bodies—exhausted from heat and want of proper food and starved for sleep. I remember nothing of that day but a dreadful consciousness of those conditions and a half-stupid realization that the day was over, and some one was encouraging me to make an effort to leave the boat and climb the steep path at Gorgona. I was assured that the worst was over, and a rest and good food at hand.

I looked at the hotel and doubted it. More pretentious than Taverneer, certainly, but all the stories I had heard before I left home of

robbery and murder at this place seemed quite
possible from the looks of the people swarm-
ing about. We were made to stop in the eat-
ing-room, as at Taverneer the night before.
until every one had a chance to eat, and I
wondered if the experience of getting to our
sleeping apartment would be repeated.

Fortunately there were stairs and beds—
really beds and bed-clothes. But sleep was
almost as hard to get as on the night before,
on account of the numbers of flying and creep-
ing things which, attracted by our light,
would swarm in the moment a door or window was opened. To sleep in a crowded room
without some place open was impossible. So
we divided up into watchers and sleepers.
While some watched the children, with the
merest ghost of a light, and did battle with
the creatures which flew or crawled in, others
snatched a little rest and sleep. The morning
light showed us many dead things that made
us shiver, slain by a vigorous hand, wielding
a woman's shoe—our only weapon.

At intervals during the night other boats
arrived, and having unloaded their passengers, the latter climbed the hill as we had
done, and were taken up in the great caravan-
sary. The noise of quarrelling and fighting

going on in the saloon and gambling-room seemed continuous, and just after midnight there was added that of the mules coming in from Aspinwall to take us over the mountain. Many of the mules had bells which kept up a tinkling sound of varied tones. The "Hoopla!" of the muleteers, the jingling of their spurs, and the delivery of every form of "cuss" words known to man, went on until every beast had his feed and every man his drink, and then silence reigned.

The silence lasted only for a short time, however,—for at the first ray of light the "Hoop-la!" rang out again and again. Kicks and oaths were delivered indiscriminately, pack-saddles were cinched, and every mule in waiting for his load. And what a sight they were! Such broken-down, miserable beasts! Hundreds of them, lame, halt, and blind, ringboned and spavined, big and little, mostly little,—everything that could be gathered up in all the country,—were brought into requisition to carry the army of people who every two weeks had to cross that mountain.

Dr. Mott had taken my order for special transportation given me by Mr. Adams, to the office at Aspinwall, and had been assured that it would be properly attended to. But as I

stood on the porch that morning and looked
at the crowd of wretched animals and the
crowd of waiting people, I wondered if it was
possible for any one to find me if they wanted
to. Some one *did* want to find me. A man
whom I had noticed as one in authority came
up to me and asked if I was the person referred
to in the order he held? The order was the
one given me by Mr. Adams. Being satisfied
that I was the right person, he asked for my
escort. I introduced Dr. Mott, and he then
took him to where he had our animals already
selected and waiting to be packed.

I have never experienced more complete
satisfaction and relief than when I saw that
little band come up for my inspection. First
were two good, strong mules for baggage, then
a riding mule for my escort, and one for our
especial muleteer, and, last of all, the dearest
pony for myself and a nice side-saddle. The
pony must have been some one's pet,—for the
gentle creature rubbed its nose on my shoul-
der and poked it into my hand, where it evi-
dently expected to find a tidbit, and treated
me altogether in a most friendly manner. Dr.
Mott's satisfaction was immense. That heavy
case of his as well as his other belongings
would be perfectly safe on that stout mule's

back. While our baggage was being packed,
we were getting ourselves ready for our ride.
Our movements were watched with the greatest interest by other parties. How we could
have such fine animals, and I a horse and side-
saddle, seemed unaccountable, and some grum-
bling was indulged in. But the agent told
all such persons that his orders came from
headquarters and had to be carried out, and
that settled the question.

My baggage fitted on the mule just as I had
arranged for it. Dr. Mott's was a load for the
other mule. He took Lena on the saddle in
front of him. I had with me a long Scotch
shawl, which the muleteer wound around
them both in such a manner as to leave them
the use of their arms, but kept her from fall-
ing off, and left him free to guide his animal.
Our two travelling bags were tied to my saddle: and so disposed we started off, in high
spirits and hopeful hearts, for our last day's
journey on land.

The gentle breeze of the mountain, so different from the sluggish and humid air which
had oppressed us on the river, seemed to make
all nature revive. Even the birds attempted
a feeble song occasionally, and the busy ants
hurried along, each with its bit of bright

flower, carried like a little sail on its back. They seemed as anxious to get somewhere as though the day were but an hour long. What did these busy creatures do with this floral burden, was a question we could not answer. Sometimes there were several lines of them going in one direction; others were returning unladen. One never wearied of watching their undulating lines as they faithfully followed their leader around a bowlder, or root of tree, or little pool of water which the frequent showers made common along the road.

Our trail lay over a spur, or high peak, and as we gradually ascended we frequently came in sight of the Chagres river far below us, bordered with huge trees, which were garlanded and festooned with brilliant flowers. Toward noon the heat became oppressive, and we were obliged to stop occasionally to give the animals a breathing-spell after a particularly tough bit of climbing.

It was after one of these rests that our first mishap occurred. When we were ready to start we missed our muleteer and baggage mules. We had been told by the agent at Gorgona never to let them out of our sight, and up to this time we had kept them in front, calling the muleteer in when he seemed in-

clined to get too far away. But now he had
got the best of us, and disappeared as completely as though the earth had opened and
taken him in. The Doctor shouted in vain,
and then rode back and forth through the
underbrush in a fruitless search which consumed much valuable time and availed nothing.

In a half-hour's ride we came upon a probable solution of the desertion. Around a large
mud-hole or pond, there were a number of
disabled mules and stranded riders. The animals, weak and tired out, would, as soon as
they came in sight of water, utterly refuse to
go farther and calmly lie down, as much of
themselves as they could in the water, and no
amount of profanity or prodding could move
them. The good woman with the eight children, who "expected to get along somehow,"
had been dumped partly in the mud, and as I
came in sight of her was dragged out, and
was being scraped off preparatory to mount-
ing another animal, when one could be found.

Some of the mules that had fallen or sat
down could not get up with their packs on,
and had them taken off and lighter ones put
on. If a good, stout mule came along which
seemed able to carry more load than he had,

he was relieved of the lighter part, and the heavy part of a weaker animal's load was put on him. Any number of these changes were made; but as we could see nothing of *our* man or mules, we moved on considerably sobered by our loss, and the Doctor nursing a great wrath against our faithless muleteer.

At noon we reached the divide, and stopped for dinner at a booth put up at the side of the trail. There was little shelter for the table in these few sticks and bushes, and a brisk wind blowing brought clouds of dust on our food, which was uninviting enough without that addition.

A boiled ham, with the mouldy skin sticking to it, a large dish of very dirty-looking boiled rice, and some chunks of black bread comprised the bill of fare. If you wanted a drink, there was a bucket of water under a tree and a gourd to drink out of; but there was not much call for water among that crowd of people. I took a little rice, but finding too much dirt in the rice, left it for a piece of bread, and got on my horse as soon as possible,—for the swarms of stinging flies made it uncomfortable to stay in the booth.

We were now going down hill all the time, and the effort to keep from going over our

animals' heads was as great as it had been
before to keep from sliding off behind. After
a while of this riding we came to a pretty
thatched cottage, with a well under a big tree
in front of it, and we thought it was just the
place for a cool drink and a rest for the animals. I did not get off my horse, but the Doctor did. He had seen a pair of bright eyes
and rosy cheeks in the cottage door, and could
not resist the temptation to air his little stock
of Spanish by making complimentary speeches
while asking for a cup to drink from.

I was smiling at his efforts, when I saw something which made me start and call quickly
for him to come to me. I said, "There is a
man watching you. Get on your mule quickly." He did not obey me a moment too soon,
—for a peon jumped from a thicket beside the
house, and but for the woman coming between
them I have no doubt he would have given
Dr. Mott something to remember, if he had
not taken his life. His knife and pistol shone
brightly in his belt, and there was an angry
gleam in his eyes.

The Doctor made good time in getting away;
and when I came up with him he was quite
willing to take a little wholesome advice,
which was to save his compliments for some

one beside Spanish women, unless he was quite
sure they had no man about.

Our descent of the mountain was much
more rapid than the ascent had been, and the
knowledge that the worst of the journey was
nearly over gave us courage to bear what was
still left to us. Now we began to see signs of
living in the increasing number of thatched
huts and paled-in bits of ground, overflowing
with fruits and vegetables. Children swarmed
around, entirely naked, and the paroquets
seemed as numerous and as much at home
as the children. They hopped on the children's heads, crawled up their legs, pecked
at their food, and made themselves quite
happy in any way which suited them. The
monkeys were also common, but not quite
as free, being usually fastened to something
about the hut.

The wonder was that children, birds, and
monkeys were not trampled under the animals' feet,— for there was no yard or fence;
all seemed to live in the road, and made no
effort to get out of our way.

About three o'clock we rode into Panama,
hot, dusty, and weary beyond expression. We
had lost so much time in looking for our baggage mules and muleteer that the greater part

of the travellers had found some sort of quarters; but there were stragglers in plenty to
keep us company, and we stopped with many
others at a long, low adobe building, labelled
"Philadelphia House." We ordered dinner,
and when it was served we sat on benches, and
I suppose must have eaten, but I can not now
recall a thing on the table.

To have to sit on a wooden bench after being in the saddle since daybreak was almost
too much to endure. After a short trial of it,
I left the table and took a seat on the broad
window-ledge, where I could look out on the
busy street and get a breath of fresh air. Soon
Lena and the Doctor joined me, and after he
had made us as comfortable as he could with
our bags and shawls, he left us to go to the
transportation office, to see if our baggage had
come in.

I sat in the window watching the strange
sights and sounds until the sun began to go
down before I realized the lapse of time.
There was an old church nearly in front of
us which was entirely covered with seashells
of nearly uniform size. In front of that was a
little house, not unlike a guardhouse, but open
on all sides except one. On that side was fastened a large font, filled with holy (?) water.

As the sun went down a chime of little bells rang out from the church tower, and immediately every man, woman, and child in the street turned toward the little house. When each one's turn came to enter in, he bent his knee, dipped his fingers in the water, and making the sign of the cross on his forehead and bosom, passed quickly out, to make way for others. Long after the bells had stopped ringing, and the twilight had come on, stragglers from the fields and laborers of all kinds came along; but no one passed by without first entering the little house and paying his slight devotions.

After it became quiet, I took Lena and went over to the church, and the witchery of the time and place was so strong upon me that I believe I should have put my fingers in the font had not the thought of those who had been there before me and the looks of the water entered a strong protest against it. But I felt so alone, so entirely apart from everything and everybody I had ever known, that for a moment the full reality of what I had undertaken came over me with an overwhelming force. I was afraid of *myself*, and ran back into the old house with a feeling of being pursued.

The daylight had lingered so long that, although it was not dark outside, I found, on
looking at my watch, that it was nearly nine
o'clock; and I felt very anxious about the
Doctor. Just then Mr. Friedlander came in.
He, too, had been at the transportation office,
looking after his baggage, and the Doctor had
asked him to tell me that one of our mules
had come in with his load all right, and he
hoped soon to get the other. He also said that
a friend of his who lived in Panama had in-
vited him to bring Lena and myself to spend
the night at his house. His wife, who was
from Boston, would be delighted to welcome
any one from there. The Doctor urged me to
hold out a little longer, and then I could have
a good night's rest in a decent house.

But the thought of staying in that place
any longer, with numbers of people of all conditions around me, was intolerable, and I
begged Mr. Friedlander to find some place
where I could be *alone*, even if I had to sit up
all night. He said that he would do his best,
but every place was so crowded, and it was so
late that it seemed almost hopeless to get anything.

After a time which seemed endless, he returned and said he had found a room—if it

could be called that — in the building next
the one we were then in; and, as there was a
white woman there who could speak English,
he really thought I had better take it. I was
too glad of anything which promised rest and
seclusion to hesitate; so I went with him. He
took Lena in his arms — by this time she was
fast asleep — and delivered us over to the servant, with many regrets that he could not do
better by us. I think, however, if he had
known that night what the daylight revealed
to me, he would have felt doubtful about leaving me there.

The room I had secured was perhaps eight
feet long and nearly as wide. The only furni-
ture in it was a cot, with no pillows or bedding, one wooden chair, and in one corner a
washstand. There was a tin wash-basin and
a broken-nosed pitcher, but no water or towels. After much coaxing and a generous tip, I
got the pitcher filled and two towels brought
me.

When the woman left, I examined my quarters. The door by which we entered seemed
to open from a very wide corridor; but, as our
light was only one candle, I could not tell
much about it. Within the room was another
door, the upper part of which was an iron

grating. Looking out of this, I saw that it
opened upon a balcony which ran around an
open court. There were trees and things down
there; but, although the moon was shining
brightly, making everything clear around
me, the court was in deep shadow, and one's
imagination could fill it with anything wild
and weird.

After making Lena as comfortable as I
could, I sat down to think what was best for
me to do. I had asked Mr. Friedlander to
tell the Doctor where I was, so that he would
be able to find me in the morning. As I had
his watch and money and a small box of val-
uables with me, I thought it possible he might
hunt me up during the night, if he got the
baggage all right. So I put my feet on the
chair, and sitting on the cot at Lena's feet, I
managed to get into a partly reclining position, using my bag for a pillow. The air was
so soft and refreshing after the heat of the day
that one did not feel the need of much cover-
ing, and my ever-serviceable shawl answered
for both of us.

About twelve o'clock the Doctor came
around to tell me that the mule with my baggage had come in, with the trunks all right;
but my bonnet-box had been taken off and

some other person's heavy trunk put in its
place. The agents were very sorry about it,
but thought that it would be put on some
other mule, and probably get in before morning. So the Doctor, leaving particular instructions to have it put with our other baggage, came to look after me. He was so sorry
to find me in such a miserable place that he
would gladly have taken me to his friend's
house, late as it was. But I was so completely
tired out that nothing could induce me to
make the change; so he gave up the idea of
going out himself, and camped somewhere in
the old house.

It seemed to me that I had only shut my
eyes again when loud talking and the sound
of many feet in the wide corridor put to flight
all thoughts of sleep. I soon found out the
cause of the commotion. The steerage passengers all walked across the Isthmus. Some
took the upper (or Cruces) trail, and others
the lower one — the same that we came over.
Travellers over both routes had arrived nearly together, and finding all the cots taken, or
not wishing to pay for one, had got permis-
sion to sleep on the balcony around the court.
From the noise they made, I thought there
were hundreds of them.

Some were so near my door that I could hear their conversation, and something caught my ear which aroused my keenest attention. They were telling some others of the men who had not been with them about a man who, they said, had been "fool enough to talk to a pretty woman" at a place where they stopped for water. He was warned against it; but having taken just enough liquor to be brave, persisted in his attention a little too long, and was stabbed to the heart by the husband, who was hiding near the house.

The man's companions at first ran away, but afterwards gathered a few new-comers, and returned to see if there was any life in him. But he was "sure enough" dead. His body was thrown aside in the bushes, and the men passed on. No one seemed to know him, and there was no time for burial. The great ship was waiting for us, and one man more or less did not count. If he had friends anywhere who looked for him, they looked in vain, and then counted him with many others who started on that perilous journey, and were left on the way, either by sickness, accident, or murder. When I told the Doctor what I had heard, he was more than ever convinced he had a very narrow escape.

I sat at my door that night while the moon lasted, looking at the ruins of churches and other buildings, which were quite near me. One had a particular fascination for me. There were four immense openings, with rounded arches joined to a wide cornice. All were overgrown with ivy, vines, and ferns, which swayed on top, or swung in the openings with every gentle breeze. When the moon left me in darkness, I made another attempt to sleep. I may have succeeded; but as the Babel of donkey-bells commenced jingling at daylight, it must have been for a very short time indeed. The steerage passengers made haste to leave the balcony and get to the ship, hoping to secure a choice of bunks.

As soon as all had gone, I looked out again for my ruin, and found it more fascinating even than during the night. The sun was gilding the towers and tree-tops, and over all were sailing in their slow, majestic flight great numbers of buzzards. I thought I had never seen anything so beautiful as their movements were,—and they were so far away I could not know they were "noisome to sight and another sense." I am glad now that I then knew nothing of their unlovely nature,—for the picture of that ruin in the morning light will remain with me as one of the most charming memories of my life.

The steamer was advertised to sail at ten o'clock, and it was nine before the Doctor made his appearance. I suppose I ought to have been anxious about him, and fearful of being left behind. But I could do nothing but wait. I think I never cared less what became of me. He hunted up the servant, and got her promise to bring me some breakfast, while he went out for one more hunt for my bonnet-box. My breakfast consisted of some black liquid in a coffee-cup and a piece of dark-looking bread. There had been sugar put in the cup, and when I stirred the liquid it gave forth such a grating sound that I concluded I did not want sweetening in mine. So, dipping the bread in the cup, we ate what we could, hoping for nothing but to sustain life until we reached the steamer.

While waiting for the Doctor, I asked the servant what kind of a house it was in which I had passed the night. She told me it had been a grand house; but when the travel became so great, with such a demand for sleeping facilities, it had been turned into one great barn-like room, filled with standees, cots, and bunks, where hundreds of men could spend the night. Only a few rooms had been left intact for the use of the family, and where I had spent the night was one of them, and seemed quite apart from the living portion of the house. It was not a pleasant situation to think over; but I was as safe probably as I am at this moment, and I doubt if any one knew a woman was there, or if they had known, would have cared. It was wholly a time of each one for himself.

At last the Doctor came for us. He had waited as long as possible, hoping to get my box, but was forced to give it up and send the other baggage out to the steamer.

I may as well give the sequel to the box affair here as elsewhere. When I arrived in San Francisco I went to Adams Express Office and reported my loss. I gave the whole history of Mr. Adams' personal efforts in getting my tickets, ordering particular transportation across the Isthmus, and the desertion of our muleteer and the loss of my box, for which I claimed three hundred dollars. I found afterward I could not have replaced its contents in California for twice that amount. They took down my statements very carefully, and on the next trip the steamer made she brought my box, which was forwarded to me many

miles in the country, with everything in it as
nice, and sweet, and safe as if it had never
been lost or strayed away. I fancy from what
Mr. Adams told me when he afterward came
to California that the transportation office in
Panama got a raking over and muleteers some
rough handling, which made baggage much
safer after that time, particularly light articles.
Before that they had been nearly all plun-
dered or stolen outright. I saw many persons
who had lost their light baggage in the same
way I had, but, unlike myself, never recovered it.

The things that impressed me most that
morning, as we made our way to the steamer,
were, first, the streets, which were *no* streets—
just a strip of ground paved with cobble-stones,
so laid as to dip toward the centre, forming a
gutter for surplus water. Then the absence
of teams,—I don't remember having seen a
vehicle of any kind. Only mules, mules everywhere! Then the absence of people, who all
seemed to have gone somewhere in the early
morning, for there were plenty of people at
that time,—some to church, others to market,
and others still to labor.

Soon we came in sight of the great steamer
lying far out in the bay. How were we to get

to it? There was no wharf or landing-place. We were now close to the water, which came up in gentle ripples near our feet. All about in the water were natives, big and little, old and young, and among these little boats were tossing idly about. Farther out, nearer the steamer, many large barges, or lighters, were hurrying along, each one trying to get its human freight first on board. I saw all this, and still thought how were we to get there? But I had learned not to ask questions!

All at once, without a word of warning, I was grabbed from behind. One black arm was around my waist, another under my knees, and I was lifted up and carried straight out into the water. I wanted to scream, but a laugh from the Doctor and a shout from Lena, who were treated the same way, changed my mind. The water deepened so gradually that it seemed a long time before we reached one of the little boats which I had looked upon as idle things, and into which we were dumped without cere- mony. One native was sufficent to row us out to one of the lighters; the others waded back to shore. Our lighter was the last to reach the steamer, and as we came up to her, there were two still to unload before our turn came.

There were no women or children on the

other boats, and only Lena and myself on ours. It was high noon, and the heat was intense. I doubted if I could live until those boats were unloaded, with that terrible sun pouring its rays on my unprotected head. Captain Patterson, who commanded the "Golden Gate," was standing at the stairs by which the passengers got on board, and seeing Lena and myself waiting in the sun, ordered one of his men to pass us over the other boats and on to the steamer.

The natives made no objection to Lena and I being so passed, but when the Doctor attempted to follow, he was set upon and held back. I heard the noise and confusion of tongues, and when I reached the top of the stairs I looked around just in time to see a native thrust his knife, as I thought, into the Doctor's heart.

A shout went out from everybody, natives, sailors, and passengers, and in an instant the offender was thrown into the water, and made to gain the shore as best he might. It was no lack of intent on his part that he did not kill when he struck, but his knife was caught on an uplifted arm, and before he could repeat the blow he was plunged into the water. Some one tied a handkerchief around the Doctor's arm, and he came up to where I was standing, looking very white, and the whole of his shirt front spattered with blood. He was taken to the surgeon's room and his arm dressed; but an artery had been cut, and he was much weakened from loss of blood.

PART III.

AT any time this sight would have been distressing to me; but my three days of exhausting travel and nights of unrefreshing sleep had so unnerved me that I could bear no more. I sank down on a coil of rope, and, although I did not faint, I was very near insensibility. I knew people were coming and going—getting settled, I supposed; but I could do nothing but wait. Lena lay on my arm, quite content to look on as long as she was with me.

After a while some one came along, and seeing me in such an uncomfortable position, took Lena and put her on a skylight, and helped me to a bench beside her. He put my shawls and bags about us, and I then felt quite indifferent as to what else might happen. The steamer had started out, and a refreshing breeze seemed to promise a chance for life again. I began to realize that the deck was gradually clearing, and that soon I would be, as once before on the "Illinois," quite alone there.

I asked the first person I saw who looked intelligent enough to deliver a straight message, to ask the purser to "please come to me." When he came I stated to him the circumstances connected with my ticket and loss of berth on the "Illinois." He heard my story, and said he would investigate. Soon he came back with the same story I had been told before,—"A party from New York had the stateroom, and would not leave it,"—but he (the purser) would give me another just as good.

I knew what that meant, and was determined I would not be imposed upon again. I asked to see the captain. The purser said all he could to persuade me to take another berth, "just while he could arrange things," he said. I insisted upon seeing the captain, and said I would wait there all night, if need be; but take any other berth than the one I was entitled to, I would not!

Finding I really meant what I said, he sent Captain Patterson to me. Again I went over the story of my ticket. He listened politely, and then asked if I had an escort or any one else who knew of the circumstances. Yes; Adams Express messenger had charge of me on the steamers. Dr. Mott took charge of me on the Isthmus. "Where were they?" The messenger was probably looking after his express matter, and Dr. Mott was the gentleman who was wounded while trying to pass me over the lighters, and had gone to the surgeon's room. The captain began to look interested. "But," I said, "there are several gentlemen on board to whom the captain of the 'Illinois' had told my trouble, and he assured them I should have my proper place on this side." When I named them, he said he would see about it and return soon, and advised me to take another berth until he had arranged matters. But I was not to be caught that way again, and declined with thanks, saying I preferred to make only one change.

It was not very long before he came back with Mr. Friedlander, who corroborated all I had said, and was quite determined to see me righted on this side, if he could do anything towards it. Again the captain offered me the use of a stateroom to rest in while he could make the changes necessary; and with Mr. Friedlander's assurance that he would take the matter into his own hands, I accepted and "retired in good order."

Oh, the luxury of clean face and hands and a change of clothing! Add to that a bowl of

clean gruel, served by a clean woman, instead
of a nasty peon, and our satisfaction was complete.

Toward evening Captain Patterson and Mr.
Friedlander again presented themselves—this
time with an attendant—to transfer our belongings to our own quarters, and for the second
time on that journey I felt I was making a
triumphant procession! Thanks to my persis-
tence, or stubbornness, my roommates on the
other side had gained their rights, and were
settled in stateroom K, first cabin, much to
their comfort and gratification. The "parties
from New York" were ousted, and none knew
whither they went.

Every one that afternoon was engaged in
a private "cleaning-up spell," but at dinner
time all were cheerful, and disposed to look
upon our troubles as being over. During the
night, however, there seemed much noise and
confusion, and next morning the breakfast
tables were comparatively deserted. We soon
learned the cause, which was that many of
our passengers had been taken sick with a
more or less serious attack of fever. Almost
every one who had eaten freely of fruit at
Panama was affected, and it seemed almost
impossible for any one to abstain when the

heat was so great and the water so bad. Many
had bought fruit and brought it on board the
steamer, partaking of it before going to bed.
Of those, I believe, none escaped the fever.

Before daylight one man died, and during
the next two days there were sixty cases of
fever and nine deaths! This state of things
was not generally known; but Dr. Holman,
the ship's surgeon, was one of the sick, and
Dr. Mott had taken his place among the patients. Of course, I knew what only a few
others did.

The day was Sunday, and it was the custom
for the captain to read a service. He thought
this a fitting time to commit "our brother"
to the deep. So we gathered on deck about
noon. The Episcopal service was read, and
some very good singing followed. Then the
body was brought out and placed on a plank
where all could see it. It had been sewn up
in a sail-cloth, and was weighted sufficiently
to insure a deep resting-place. The service for
burial at sea was read, and then the wheels
were stopped. The men uncovered their heads,
the plank was tipped over the side, and a
splash of water told the rest.

It is safe to say that of those who witnessed
this ceremony all who were at all indisposed

took to their berths and were very sure they
had the fever. The well ones told the sick of
this scene, and before night there was such an
alarming increase of new patients, and the
old ones were so much worse, that the captain
and doctors held a consultation and decided
upon a different course. The sick were iso-
lated as much as possible. We were told everybody was getting well and that nobody died.
This view of the case really had a good effect
and lessened the terror of the fever.

After this when a soul passed away nothing
was said about it, and when night came on
the ocean received the body, and not so much
as one revolution of the wheel was stayed.
This was the easier done from the fact that
a majority of the sick, and I believe all who
died, were steerage passengers, and had no
one to particularly care for them. Of the
saloon and stateroom passengers, all recovered
after a few days' illness; but I believe the
malarial symptoms would recur years after.
One doctor stoutly maintained that if a person once had Panama fever it was never wholly
eradicated from the system.

Lena and I escaped entirely, and I believe
it was due to caution in eating and drinking.
We drank no water unless in tea or coffee and

ate no fruit except oranges, and these only in
the morning before breakfast. They were a
great thin-skinned, delicious fruit, and we were
never without them.

By the time we reached Acapulco, where we
stopped to coal, there were no new cases of
fever, and most of the old ones were in a fair
way to recovery.

At Acapulco were many people who made
great efforts to get on our steamer. There had
been a shipwreck ninety miles below, and of
those who were saved many had reached that
place, and were now very anxious to get on
some vessel going to San Francisco. We had
been from the first very much crowded, but
I am sure we saw many strange faces after
we left that port.

While we were lying there, the captain came
to the ladies' saloon with a pitiful story of a
woman who had been shipwrecked, and was
now at Acapulco, so very sick that the Sisters
had taken her to the convent and were trying
to save her life. The person who had charge
of her had been to Captain Patterson, and
begged him to take her on his steamer, as he
was sure she would never recover in that hot
climate. There was no stateroom, or even
berth, unoccupied; but the captain said there

could be a place made for her in our saloon, if we did not object. No one did object; but it was not a pleasant prospect to have a person in our sight who might die at any moment. However, she was brought in on a mattress,—and I never saw a living being look so deathly. One good soul on board saw her doleful state, and gave up his stateroom to her. She was moved into it the next morning. From the moment she came on board she began to mend, and before we reached San Francisco was comparatively well. She afterward married Mr. Peck, of the firm of Wellman, Peck & Co., and became rather notable in connection with a long lawsuit involving her husband's estate, which she gained but did not live long to enjoy.

The day after we left Acapulco the captain had some trouble with one of the stowaways, who had got on, no one knew how, at that place. The man had been ordered to do something and had not obeyed with the alacrity desirable on shipboard, for which he was sent to the coal-hole. If there is any hotter place than a coal-hole on a steamer in the tropics, mortals have not yet found it, or a way to live in it, and this poor fellow quietly lay down and died after a few hours' trial.

Some one saw the man lying there, and reported to the captain. He said the man was probably shamming, and ordered a whipping unless he went on with his work. The man did not mind that a bit, and persisted in being dead, which seemed to irritate the captain, and made him think something really ought to be done about it. So that night he got the doctors together, and they made a *post mortem* examination and found it was a case of brain fever! Probably had it when he came on board!

This was the verdict of two physicians, made out in proper form and duly signed, as I understood, for future reference, in case any question arose about the man's death. The passengers' verdict was a little different, being that the man died of hunger and thirst in a coal-hole in the tropics.

This was our last unpleasant experience. The sea was calm, the nights beautiful. While the moon lasted, we would go on the wheel-house and watch the phosphorescent light on the water, looking as if we were in reality sailing over a silver sea. The sight would charm us into silence for a while; then some one would hum a tune, one and another would fall in with some old-fashioned air, and we would wind up with all sorts of tunes, or no tune at all.

During the day how delightfully lazy we were! Those of us who had a bit of embroidery about thought we worked some, but the result was not worth mentioning. Every day some incident arose in our little world which caused as much gossip as though we were on land and had our daily paper. I will say this much in our favor: there were no quarrels or bickerings, which I was told was very unusual, and we rather dreaded the breaking up of our pleasant intercourse.

We had only one rough day on this side. While passing Cape St. Lucas we were beaten and banged about in a rough sea, just as we were going down for breakfast. Some returned to their berths, and others persisted in their efforts to dress, with varying success. Others still, who felt like the canny Scot who had "contracted for his food" and meant to get his money's worth, went to breakfast only to fight their way on deck again, and set down that meal to account of profit and loss.

Sometimes we saw a sail at a distance, and again a school of porpoises. Anything, everything, little or big, caused a rush on deck and animated discussion or exchange of opinion.

But as we neared the end of our journey, all other interests were swallowed up in the one anxiety of how much were we going to beat all former records. Twenty-five days was the shortest time in which the trip had been made; but Captain Patterson had said he thought the "Illinois" and "Golden Gate," being then the two fastest boats running together, could make it in twenty days, or in twenty-two at the outside.

Now, as we sighted San Diego, we realized it was to be no twenty days' trip for us, and some bets were made as to how much less than the twenty-five days' record we should make. San Diego seemed a place of great interest to everybody. It was the first land in sight, and to those who had been to California before was as dear to their hearts as though their lives had been spent there. But it was "Old California! Hurrah and hurrah! for the bang-upest place in the whole world!" Every glass was brought out and levelled at what was supposed to be San Diego; but as the captain's desire was to keep as far out to sea as he could consistently with his proper course, I doubt if many of those who so persistently glued their eyes to their glasses really saw the land. But it was "San Diego" and "San Deago" and

"San Daigo" all day, every individual using a pronunciation to suit himself.

When the "Golden Gate" went down to Panama for us, she had taken San Francisco papers, which had been sought after with the greatest interest. There had been an election of some kind, and followers of both parties were on our ship. Two nights before we arrived, every stateroom seemed to be holding a political meeting. Speeches, hurrahs, and songs made sleep impossible. I do not know in the least what it was all about. One of the songs was of that kind where there are any number of verses made to order, and the chorus —in which everybody joined—was, "And Solomen Heydenfeldt!" This seemed to please both parties immensely, and hearty cheers always followed its utterance.

We reached San Francisco in the evening of the twenty-third day out—beating all other records by two and a half days, which, if not all we wished, was a *beat*, anyhow. A pilot-boat came out, bringing papers, which were eagerly sought by those who knew anything of the country. For us who were strangers a quiet night's rest seemed the best preparation for the new life we were to begin the next day. I do not know if any one else slept. I know

I did not, but am only telling one woman's experience, and how she felt about it.

We lay out in the bay that night, and the next morning steamed up to the wharf in the bright and beautiful sunshine. The strangest sight then was the forest of dismantled ships. It seemed to me there were hundreds of them, and their blackened spars cut out sharply against the blue sky without a particle of canvas on them. The ships had been deserted by their crews, and the sails taken for tents, either here or carried into the mines. They were a sorry sight, lying there so idly fretting their lives away. Very few ever floated a canvas again, but became "old hulks," or were converted into storehouses. Some were run up on the flats as far as possible, and served as foundations for buildings in locations now considered the heart of the city.

As soon as we landed I sent some letters which I had brought with me to their addresses. Sooner than I could have thought possible, Caleb T. Fay answered one of them in person. He took us to the Rassette House, where I was to wait for messages from the country. He treated me in the kindest manner, and during my three days' stay there I had few lonely hours, which but for his kindness I might have had, as Lena was quite sick, and I could not take her out or leave her in the house without me.

When I entered my room that first day I went to the window, which was a front one and near the centre of the building, and looked up the street a distance which seemed a few blocks away. There all vestige of a street vanished, and the rickety fences ended in a sand heap. I thought, "Can this ever be a city?" And yet the spot where my eyes rested that morning has been my well-beloved home for thirty-two years!

No longer a sand-heap surely—but pleasant and accessible beyond most parts of the city.

When I left Boston, I said, "No; I will never go backward!" I have kept my word, and no shadow of regret has ever found a lodgment in my heart for my venture. If days were dark, I would rather have them here than elsewhere, and if bright, they were all the brighter for being in California.

www.ingramcontent.com/pod-product-compliance
Lightning Source LLC
Chambersburg PA
CBHW020333090426
42735CB00009B/1519